So She Did

Molly Stocks

BookLeaf
Publishing

India | USA | UK

So She Did

© 2021 Molly Stocks

All rights reserved.

No part of this publication may be reproduced, stored in a retrieval system, or transmitted, in any form or by any means, electronic, mechanical, photocopying, recording or otherwise, without the prior written permission of the presenters.

Molly Stocks asserts the moral right to be identified as the author of this work.

Presentation by *BookLeaf Publishing*

Web: www.bookleafpub.com

E-mail: info@bookleafpub.com

ISBN : 9789358361124

First edition 2021

ACKNOWLEDGEMENT

To my friends and family who supported me.Also to My dog Lady who gave me many smiles and heard every poem.

Grade A

Words turn into Gossip

All to get a scholarship

Books turns to looks Everything is a
popularity test

But don't be stressed

You need to rest Get an A on that test

Like I do for all the rest

Not mentally okay

Stress spinning through my brain

Is it going to be okay?"

Darken Heart

Heart broken

Shattered like glass

Love is not for the class

Talk of the town

Did you hear?

Lies the rumours always near

Love is one sided

Switch it on and switch it off

Keep your heart on a lock

The love of soulmates

It's just a bait

To catch a fish

Is just a trait A heart of gold

Not ready to be hold

Now is old

It's all a game

That you replay

Until the heart is dark

Like my lerking past With every game
played

It's like another wave

Until it is darken to black again

Like the old games we play

But love for someone special will blind
you Will darken the heart and soul

For Enternity

Daisy

A flower crown

Ready for a bow

Smells so sweet

It can't be beat Dancing in a daisy chain

Flowing and swaying

Singing daisy as the wind is blowing

Every year it grows again

It glows in the light

Ties together like a beautiful bow

Standing on a peaceful field

It creates happiness on every face

Like a peice of lace

The daisy smile for further more"

Reality check

World put on pause

All if its flaws

Grabs you with its claws

Wish we could applause

All stuck in a jail

Time goes like a snail

But do not wail

The world is dying

Stop the lying

We need to start trying

To save the world

We need to stand together

Let's keep the connections

Like we did in this pandemic

To keep this world epic

For the next generation"

Horses

The love of a horse

The love of the outdoors

Ally's future horse that she adores.

There is no more chores

Money in her purse

The future is secure

She is fierce

On a world tour

As they explore

Last Words

Love is love

Like a dove

But don't take advantage

The written words are his last

But his words are never in the past

His work is not a draft

Everyone is in the work

To show all our glory

Be forever in the last words"

Golden gates

Spell of love

Won't be in vain

Like the rain

It's never ending circle

Will live forever

They belong to the golden gates

To the souls

Who Believe"

Trapped

Young girls are told

Not to be bold

They are trapped

 There are locked

Stuck in a jail

They are trapped

But don't forget about that lap

Stay fit

Look pretty

Fit the styles

All trapped

Everyday is a trap

Family

It is tough

It is fun

Know when to run

So you can leave the nest

Be happy

Who ever your family

If that's freinds

If that books

Reality or fiction

We still love

Talking

We talk for days

Look across the bay

To see your smile.

We miss our talks

As we are in the moment

Just talking

Watching the years go bye

We remember

The memories of our talks

By long gone days

Life

We start small

Then we grow tall

As we grow

We learn to laugh

To smile

To catch a dream

So memories

Dreams

Stay with us

Duck

Look at the duck

That is lucky to be seen

In the morning

To see the snow

See it glow

The duck stands tall

With each smile

It sees.

Full Of Hope

All around us

As we get the bus

Or cleaning the dust

It will bring. Hope

Of a new day

Dreams shine so bright

As we see the hope

Bad News

We think

And think

Plays again

Again

Hoping it will go

Feel so low

Even with hope

But

Good news

Will come

Dogs

How crazy

Chasing flies

They are best friend

Not just for man

But for all

As the make us smile

Memories last forever

Of our beloved

Dogs.

Steps

Take it slow

We will get there

In the end

As we climb the ladder

To pay the rent

Take it slow

The steps are hard

Write the card

Showing your next step

Cats

Cats

Rhymes with bat's

Both independent

Some are mischievous

Some are funny

But it doesn't matter

What they do.

We love them

Even with the war

Between cats and dogs.

Secrets

We hold tight

People bite there tounge

To keep the peace

As secrets

Become gossip

Become happiness

Into peace

Into drama

Into peace

Secrets is the beginning and the end

In the circle of secrets

World

Protect

Magical

Hope for the younger

For the future

Will this world survive

Is up to us

As we protect

Are miracle world

The world

Outside

Trees

The bees

Makes peace

As the fields run

No pollution

From the dump

As sunset shows

Like rows

The outside flows

Happy

Smiles that fill the room

I am with them

The moment

Is ours

No matter which

Is happy or sad.

But the moment feels great

When we are together

And happy.

Dancing

In the morning

In the sun

In the snow

In the rain

We flow into the music

As we dance

Intelligent

We rate

It's like bait

We do not need

Knowledge

Time

Money

Is all we need

Intelligent scales

Should be in the past.

Merlin Crafts

Started small

As we grow

Crafts fill the room

As the flowers bloom

Items selling

Keyrings

Cards

Dreams appeared one

At a time.

Love

It came

It went

Like a shooting star

It's here

It's gone

A wish of true love

Is a maze

With one wish

This is love.

Art

The panting glows

As we admire

Hard work is shown

In every piece

Art can be small

Or big

Interesting or boring

Artists show their art.

Keep Going

Try and make it

Possibilities

Everywhere you look

None are took

As we keep moving

Sometimes fast

Sometimes slow

But we keep going.

Time

Is running out

As we shout

As it goes to fast

We can not catch

As we try

Time gets further away

As it runs out

Time.

Ready

Are you ready for change

Are you ready for challenge

Are u ready of what comes ahead

Is it a dream

Or are you ready to fight

Show them the light

If you are ready.

Best Friends

We love them

We care for them

We have fun

No matter the distance

From the start

Like a dart

We are there when we can

As we are best friends

Warriors

Watch as we run

For fun

Don't catch up

Your on watch

As we fight

For a dream

To look back

To see you again

Our hope

With every warrior.

Colour

Splash the page

Happy

Sad

Anger

Of our soul

Of our dreams

All comes

With a colour